William Woty

Fugitive And Original Poems

William Woty

Fugitive And Original Poems

ISBN/EAN: 9783744709453

Printed in Europe, USA, Canada, Australia, Japan

Cover: Foto ©Thomas Meinert / pixelio.de

More available books at **www.hansebooks.com**

FUGITIVE

AND

ORIGINAL

POEMS.

By W. WOTY, Gent.

Price THREE SHILLINGS.

PRINTED FOR THE AUTHOR, BY J. DREWRY, DERBY,

M,DCC,LXXXVI.

The STAGE.

An Epistle to a Friend.

—————

YES, with an iron Rod you lash the Stage,

Forgetting, that in this you lash the Age,

Drawcansir like, exhaust without Regard,

Your wrath on Actor, Manager, and Bard.

But tho' their Conduct harshly you defame,

Candor dares vouch, that neither is to blame.

Such as the Congress are, who hear and see,

Will Actor, Manager, and Author be.

'Tis

'Tis public Taſte, that ever muſt controul,

The Drama's motions, and direct the whole.

Sterling, or baſe, as that may chance to prove,

Th' accordant Currency will ſtop, or move.

Through balmy meadows, fring'd with many a flow'r

Where friendly Nature ſheds her fertile ſhow'r,

The muddy ſtream creeps ſluggiſhly along,

Too dull to animate the Poet's ſong;

At this you wonder—but vouchſafe to tread

Your footſteps backwards to the fountain's head,

Limpid, or foul, the ſtream will be the ſame,

True to the faithful Urn, from whence it came.

Alike it fares with thoſe, who write or play:

They muſt conſult the Mirror of the day,

Adapt

Adapt their looks to Fashion's glaring light,
No matter, if the glaſs be wrong, or right.

Unhappy he! to pleaſe a childiſh Age,
Who waſtes his parts, and Credit on the Stage,
Forc'd to expoſe the Trinkets of the mind,
And leave the gems, the precious gems behind.
Genius no more then darts his dazzling rays,
But lies, ſweet *Nonſenſe!* ſmother'd in thy blaze.

THOU! darling of the Times! to thee belong
The Eunuch's warble, and unmanly ſong,
The turgid Tragedy of ahs! and ohs!
Where not one ſpark of genuine Nature glows,
Cold Comedy, that ſomething *would* expreſs,
Where Humour freezes in Tranſlation's Dreſs,

While

Whilft Wit, whofe glance once awed the Villain's pride,

Drops the dead eye, and ftiffens by her fide.

The mighty Range of SHAKESPEARE's god-like mind,

Who left e'en Nature in the Race behind,

That, like a doting Mother ftop'd, and fmil'd,

Pleas'd to be vanquifh'd by her fondling Child.

The varied Notes of DRYDEN's magic lyre,

Whofe founds harmonious fet the Soul on fire;

The plaintive ftrains of OTWAY's tender Mufe,

Who could at will foft pity's warmth infufe,

From favage eyes the trickling Sorrow fteal,

Strike on the Nerves, and make the Heart-ftrings feel,

Ill-fated bard !—the happy thoughts that flow

In liquid language from enchanting ROWE,

The fire, and Senfibility of LEE,

Whofe Beauties clafs him in the firft degree,

Whofe

Whofe daring Courfer, when the common track

He fpurn'd at random, always brought him back,

With other Spirits of illuftrious Fame

Well-known, and needlefs for the Mufe to name,

Thefe are no more.   The Public form the twine

Of Bays for *Harlequin* and *Columbine*,

To Wit and *Congreve* farce and fong prefer,

As if on purpofe they defign'd to err,

Humour and *Vanbrugh* muft give place to Sound,

Such is the trifling Tafte in Folly's Round.

See! where the Fools of Quality appear,

Whofe Underftanding centres in the Ear.

Charm'd with the Trills of an *Italian* throat,

As if they knew the language and the Note,

They dance their empty Noddles to and fro,

Enough for them, poor things! to feem to know.

In vain for them the Tear of pity flows,

They cannot taste imaginary Woes.

'Tis real Grief alone, that dews their eyes

When colic-sick a fav'rite lap-dog lies.

But that's allay'd, when proof of high regard !

They first receive the dear, condoling Card.

The Servant runs the Doctor's Aid to beg,

But in returning falls, and breaks his Leg.

Ne'er mind the Leg, my Lord and Lady cry,

If *Celsus* comes, and *Pompey* does not die.

But far more pungent griefs their frames assail,

When Scandal ceases, and when Parties fail,

When Dissipation's lazy Wheel stands still,

And something thwarts their pow'r of acting ill,

When Pleasure proves to their Addresses coy,

And Disappointment curbs the Rein of Joy.

What

What Bard would write, when such the Judges are!

What skilful Actor his Exertions dare!

Vain may the Actor and the Poet join,

And like true friends, their mutual force combine.

If but a *Veſtris* ſhake his agile toe,

Or fops import ſome foreign Raree-ſhow,

Who will for them, to Senſe of feeling dead,

May take a SHAKESPEARE's or a GARRICK's Head.

SHADE of the former! pardon, when I join

His favor'd Name in the ſame Verſe with thine.

In all thy Scenes that dignify the Stage,

His Action beſt explain'd thy matchleſs page.

One look from him convey'd thy Meaning more,

Than all the Notes thy Critics had in ſtore.

And

And let not here the rigid man of phlegm

Rafhly the Players, or the Plays condemn.

Is there an Actor, who fuftains his part

With blamelefs conduct, deftitute of Art,

In private life, maintaining Virtue's caufe,

No Actor here—that man deferves Applaufe.

Some fuch there are, whofe felf-approving hour

Tranfcends the limit of the Mufe's pow'r.

But tho' the Actor and the Poet join,

Walk hand in hand to Fame's immortal fhrine,

Death parts their friendly travel in the end,

Nor gives their fhining Talents more to blend.

Frefh round the Poet's grave the Laurel grows,

And o'er his Turf a pleafing fhadow throws,

Whilft o'er the Actor's perifhable Tomb,

A wither'd Cyprefs only marks his Doom.

His

His Charms the one continues to renew,

And one is clos'd for ever from the View.

Of this no more—the Time may yet revive

To keep Pit, Box, and Gallery alive,

When Posture-masters may distort the frame,

Screw up their Limbs, and tumble into fame,

When some may swing upon the flexile wire,

And some, a match for *Vulcan*, swallow fire.

Monkies may dance to please the human flock,

And triumph o'er the Buskin, and the Sock.

Rouze! Britons, rouze! and banish from the Scene,

Dumb shows, and noise, the frivolous, and mean;

The useful Stage we then may hope to see,

The School of Virtue, as it ought to be.

C

Strike

Strike out the Thoughts from ev'ry Author's page

Pen'd but to pleafe a loofe, abandon'd Age,

Where can more noble Sentiments be found?

In perfect Unifon the Senfe and Sound,

Where punifh'd Vice in anguifh bites the Earth,

And Folly flinches at the fhaft of Mirth,

Where Virtue fmiles, nor knows a fingle fear,

And Pity gives to Grief the healing tear,

Where comes Inftruction, and the more to pleafe,

Comes in the veftment of poetic eafe,

Where Truth fublime, defcending from the fky,

Expands her Book of Ethics to the eye,

Where, ftrengthen'd by the fage Hiftorian's mind,

Stands broad to view, the Volume of Mankind.

Nor let grave Priefts, whom I to all prefer,

When Meeknefs marks their facred Character,

Nor

Nor let grave Priests the Mufe prophane efteem,

Tho' fhe has chofen this unhallow'd Theme.

For next the Pulpit doth a virtuous Stage

Convey the pureft Leffons to the Age.

But Reformation can the Stage expect!

When thofe, who ought to patronize, neglect.

Where 'mongft the Great in Education's Sphere

Doth Ormond, Dorset, Hallifax appear!

Thofe Orbs of Tafte, beneath whofe ample blaze

Dryden fhone forth with more illumin'd rays.

True Genius then majeftically dar'd

Enough to frighten ev'ry modern Bard,

That, like a mighty flood with fury fraught,

Roll'd the refiftlefs Cataract of Thought,

Tho' now it flows an even, paffive ftream,

To welcome Slumber, and invite the dream.

True

True Genius, tho' inhum'd, lives after death
When all the Critics have refign'd their breath.
His fame furviving ftill does DRYDEN keep,
And POPE's awake, tho' *Dennis* is afleep.

But now no Patrons raife the Poet's head,
Or call forth Merit from her humble fhed.
A coaxing Proftitute, or fparkling Toy,
Almoft completes the fummit of their Joy.

Our Nobles now to Climes exotic roam,
And travel, but to travel from their home.
They pay their Vifits to the Continent,
Returning juft as wife, as when they went.
No more—unlefs to bring a Toothpick back,
Or fome important, lufory Knick-knack;

Perhaps

Perhaps a Cookling to debauch the Tafte,

And let their Wealth, and Kitchens run to wafte,

Or half-ftarv'd Wretch his Friends could not endure

To drefs their flimfy pates—a pert Frifeur.

Afk them the Hift'ry—Cuftoms of a place,

Confus'd they ftare with an infipid face,

But talk of Sing-fong, and of Opera dance,

The *Gamut's* all the learning they advance.

Are thefe the Men to rule the public tafte?

If fo, the Stage will not reform in hafte.

Actors full oft, tho' not with much delight,

Have blufh'd to fpeak, what Authors blufh'd to write.

You'll archly afk this Queftion, friend, I fear:

Pray did the Boxes never blufh to hear?

O no—they love fweet Nonfenfe it is known,

As bord'ring near a province of their own,

Or

Or fhould they blufh, the Colour is fo faint,

You fcarce can fee it through the Veil of Paint.

Till Education purifies the Mind,

Of thofe, who ought to civilize Mankind,

Men of exalted Rank, whofe ample Worth

Should keep due pace with their exalted Birth,

The Stage muft in its motley ftate remain,

A Proof, that Tafte hath not fecur'd her Reign,

Whilft Senfe is hifs'd, and Acclamation rings

The praife of gew-gaws, and of fiddle-ftrings.

To the MEMORY of the late
CHARLES CHURCHILL.

———

THERE was a time, when *Churchill's* nervous muse,

The genuine Strain of Satire cou'd diffuse,

Drag Vice and Folly from their lurking Cave,

And Justice plauded ev'ry stroke she gave ;

When guilty Statesmen, of no common Note,

Crouch'd at his Name, and trembl'd as he wrote,

When he stood forth with firm, and honest Zeal,

Ne'er to be bias'd from the public Weal,

Of English Rights the Advocate and Guard,

And Admiration hail'd the daring Bard.

This is the Time for those, by Rancor led,

Who prais'd him living, to abuse him dead.

But

But who immortal praifes can infure,

When POPE, harmonious POPE is not fecure!

When W——n, ftudious more to damn, than fave,

Meanly attacks, and flogs him in the Grave.

So fares it, CHURCHILL, with thy honor'd Name,

Which ftill fhall echo from the Trump of Fame.

Let puny Witlings, felf-conceited Elves,

Who never think, or reafon for themfelves,

But take their Sentiments on Truft alone,

And from another's Judgement form their own,

Deny thee Fancy, Numbers too deny,

To fuch thy GOTHAM roundly gives the Lie.

There Fancy braids a Wreath of curious hue,

And dips the leaves in pure Caftalian dew,

Then with a look, un-ruffl'd by a Frown,

Around Defcription's Temples binds the Crown,

Who

Who nobly fpurning Coxcomb Fafhion's laws,

With grace untaught attracts our juft Applaufe.

Nor lefs in FAMINE doth fhe charm the eye,

Which none but angry Scotfmen, will deny,

Tho' there fhe is conftrain'd to change her drefs,

But in that Change fhe pleafes not the lefs.

The Portrait of the Hag fhall fix'd remain,

And Envy ftrive to gnaw it out in vain.

Her loathfome Cave, that never Sun-fhine knew

And like herfelf, moft frightful to the View,

Shall ftrike each wand'ring Traveller aghaft

While Efts, Slugs, Toads, and hiffing Serpents laft.

What man, who reads thy NIGHT, but muft admire,

The Strength of Language, and the Thought of Fire!

D   And

And tho' its blaze may fometimes ceafe to fhine,

A Fervor iffues from thy coldeft Line.

To thofe, who wrapt in foft Arcadian dreams,

Lull'd by the lapfe of flow-meand'ring ftreams,

Fond of fome rural Nymph of beauteous frame,

Whom they diftinguifh'd by a claffic Name,

Who ftudied, to obtain the meed of praife,

The terfe expreffion, and the florid phrafe,

To weeping Willows told a rueful Tale,

And burthen'd with their fighs the gentle gale,

Thy manly fpirit ne'er could condefcend,

In token of Affent the knee to bend,

But left indiff'rent, without Love or Hate,

Such wifhy-wafhy Foplings to their Fate.

Thy ſubjeĉts, local as they are, contain

A rich, poetic, and a laſting Vein;

And ſure, 'tis harder of the two, to keep

A local ſubjeĉt from Oblivion's ſleep,

Than gen'ral Themes, which will exiſt of courſe,

Without th' exertion of the Poet's force.

With ſoul undaunted did'ſt thou bravely dare,

To hurl defiance at the Critic's Chair,

To mount in Triumph the Parnaſſian Throne,

And keep thy Seat, thyſelf a Hoſt in one.

On

On a certain DUKE'*s feeming to undervalue the* LORD

CHANCELLOR *in an auguft Affembly on his new-*

created Peerage.

WITH founding Titles, and illuftrious Birth,

Doth Senfe defcend, or all-accomplifh'd Worth!

If not, ye long-lin'd Great! forbear to fneer,

Or caft reflections on a modern Peer.

The Peer to day is as completely fo,

As Peers, who fprung from Peers fome years ago.

Who founds a Family on Merit's Bafe,

Stands he not nobler than the poftern Race!

They but inherit, what the other got,

And what the Merit of Succeffion—What!

Vain of defcent, who proudly rears his Head,

Leans on the fplendid Crutches of the dead,

A

A borrow'd prop—tho' parts and lineage join,

Creation ſtamp'd the Value on the Coin,

And Kings with Joy the firſt Impreſſions gave,

To worthy Minds—the virtuous and the brave.

Some few Exceptions may admit excuſe,

But thoſe let G——n's mighty ſelf produce.

On, THURLOW, on! to conſcious Right awake,

For Vice will ſhrink, when Virtue dares to ſpeak.

Alike will Folly tremble, and recede,

When Truth appears, and Knowledge lifts her Head.

On, THURLOW, on! whoſe able Spirit charms,

Whoſe Juſtice quickens, and whoſe firmneſs warms,

Tho' cautious, manly, humble, yet not mean,

Conciſe, yet copious, dauntleſs, tho' ſerene.

Accept this Homage from an honeſt Muſe,

Nor ſlight her Viſit, tho' ſhe brings no News.

✙·✙·✙·✙

On the BEAUTY and UTILITY of
COCK - FIGHTING.

G AY Chanticleer to adolescence grown,

For high descent, and lineal courage known,

At length is render'd to the Feeder's hand,

First in the list of the plebeian Band.

A *Genius He*, if Fame aright records,

Rever'd by Gentlemen, rever'd by Lords.

Nor less the Parson owns his mighty skill,

And the crop'd Curate cringes to his Will.

Him too the sapient Doctor eyes with glee,

And, strange to tell! almost forgets his fee.

Nor wonder, if the Lawyer join the Train,

The more Contention—still the more his Gain.

Tag, rag, and bob-tail mingle in the throng,

Sure to be right, 'till sure they have been wrong.

All,

All, one and all, unanimously join,

Quit their own Orbs in other Orbs to shine.

Hail happy Feeder! thou, who can'ft engage

The deep Attention of a knowing age!

To thee they bow, and on thy Words rely,

As Dupes on Sharpers, whose vile Ware they buy.

To thee tho' Science never oped her Lock,

Enough for thee the Science of a Cock.

Tis thine to fweat him, weapon, trim, and try,

For the grand end—to conquer, or to die.

The day of Battle come, the folemn day

To entertain the rabble of the Fray.

The Circus opens, and with accent loud

In rufh precipitate the motley Croud,

Noble,

Noble, ignoble, a promiſcuous Train,

To ſee a pleaſure, ſome would call a pain.

Anxious they wait each doughty Chieftain's nod,

The Maſters, and Comptrollers of the Sod.

The Combatants are pitch'd—the pit reſounds,

And all the Scene is nought, but blood and wounds.

The ſtately Birds, Aurora's Harbingers,

Are hack'd, and mangl'd with each others ſpurs.

With gore half-choak'd, one peeps with half an eye,

And one hops limping with a broken thigh,

Convuls'd and agoniz'd at ev'ry pore,

At length they ſtrike at once, and fall to riſe no more.

O glorious ſport, and worthy Britain's race!

And oh! how far ſuperior to the Chace!

Youth's

Youth's beſt Academy ! where all may learn,

Things of important moment, and concern,

To feel Compaſſion for another's woe,

And burn, or freeze, at each repeated blow.

The martial Hero here ſo prim and pert,

May learn his Colors never to deſert,

But nobly fight it to his lateſt breath,

And ſeek renown in honorable death.

Noting the Betts, the odds, and turns of Chance,

The 'Prentice ſoon in figures may advance,

And ſet his father down an arrant fool,

For ſo much Waſte in ſending him to School.

Of all the Books, which once could ſtand the Teſt,

Cocker's Arithmetic was judg'd the beſt.

But here that Science is more early taught,

More ably learn'd, and with leſs labor bought.

E   What

What a rare School of Harmony is here!

What magic Sounds bewitch Attention's ear!

Did ever Handel's Notes with more controul

Arreſt, affect, and agitate the Soul!

Did ever Cicero's correct harangue

Rival this flowing Eloquence of *Slang*.*

The tragic Actor here may learn to ſtart,

And catch the ſhifting paſſions of the Heart,

The dark ſuſpence, the terrible Surprize,

The brow's grim frown, and Fury of the eyes.

Whate'er, like Art, may on the ſtage appear,

Is but the ſtroke of genuine Nature here.

Long as the Painter's colors ſhall ſurvive,

Long as Engravers keep their Art alive,

Duckwing and *Ginger* ſhall be handed down,

Diſtinguiſh'd on the page of fair renown.

Yes—

* A cant Word for vulgar language.

Yes—their high Names ſhall ſtand without a blot,

When thoſe, who own'd and fed them, are forgot.

In this gay ſcene no Compliment is paid,

To Youth, Age, Birth, Nobility, or Trade.

All are co-equal, as one common Soul,

One level principle directs the whole.

So at ſome droll Election have I ſeen,

Perſons unite, as various as their mien,

The high, the low, in ſtrange confuſion meet,

And Lords with Coblers hiccup in the ſtreet,

Nor, which was which, could any Mortal gueſs,

The Cobler, or the Lord, but from his dreſs.

SONG.

SONG.

I.

ZEPHYR! with thy downy Wing,

 Sweep the bosom of each flow'r;

Mingl'd odors hither bring,

 Delia sleeps within the Bow'r.

II.

Delia sleeps—but still denies

 Respite to her Lover's smart,

Chaces slumber from his eyes,

 Pours fresh Anguish on his Heart.

III.

See! the trembling leaves beneath

 Active sports th' obsequious Air.

          Hark!

Hark! Æolian founds that breathe

Harmony to lull the Fair.

IV.

Slumb'ring Pride now drops her Shield;

Dream! thy foft enchantment prove,

Make the Nymph to Fancy yield

Tranfports fhe refus'd to Love.

BISHOP

BISHOP LOWTH's LINES

ON HIS

DECEAS'D DAUGHTER.

CARA vale! ingenio præstans, pietate, pudore,

    Et plufquam Natæ nomine, cara vale!

Cara Maria, vale! at veniet felicius œvum,

    Quando iterum tecum fim, modo dignus ero.

Cara redi! læta tum dicam voce, paternos,

    Eja age in amplexus, cara Maria, redi!

TRANSLATION.

I.

Adieu! thou darling of my vital frame!

So polifh'd, holy, modeft, and fo true,

Still more engaging in a Daughter's Name,

Thou darling of my vital frame, adieu!

II.

Adieu, Maria! but a happier Time,

I truſt, will come to ſooth a Father's pain,

When, heav'n-ward, I may wing my flight ſublime,

And gaze on loſt Maria's Charms again.

III.

Diſſolv'd in Tranſport, then ſhall I exclaim,

My Sweet! for whoſe belov'd embrace I burn,

Dear and more dear, thou innocent of blame!

Return, Maria! to my Arms return!

To a LADY, *who has written an excellent Poem on*
REVEAL'D RELIGION, *and through Diffi-*
dence withholds it from Publication.

AS far fecluded from the Realm of Tafte,

Like *Venus* beauteous, and like *Dian*, chafte,

Some rural Nymph difplays her prime of Youth,

And notic'd only by the Swain uncouth,

But when in bright, accomplifh'd Circles feen,

All wonder at the lovely ftranger's mien,

Surpriz'd, that fo much Beauty fhould fo long

Have lain conceal'd amidft a ruftic Throng.

So thy fweet Mufe, in modeft robe array'd,

In vain her fplendid image hath difplay'd,

Travers'd the paths of dull Recefs too long,

And breath'd with fervor her celeftial fong,

That

That song, whofe Notes, fo mufically foft,

Might draw an Angel downward from aloft.

Dare then to bring her to the public view,

To take that praife, which is fo much her due,

Envy confounded fhall her quill fufpend,

And ev'ry Critic prove MARIA's friend.

F   EPITAPH

EPITAPH ON
Doctor JOHNSON.

YE vain licentious Wits! your diſtance keep,

And, if you never wept, now learn to weep.

Learning hath loſt her Prop in JOHNSON's End,

Virtue her boaſt, and Piety her Friend.

Preſume not to this Shrine too near to draw,

Or, if you dare approach, approach with Awe.

The Scythe of Time ſhall canker o'er with Ruſt,

Loſe its keen edge, and ſplinter into Duſt;

Himſelf too ſicken, and in Anguiſh pine,

Ere he ſhall gain a Harveſt ſo divine.

But tho' thy form be ſnatch'd from mortal eye,

JOHNSON! thy ſpotleſs fame ſhall never die.

Clos'd as thou art in Death's eternal Cave,

Thy Works ſhall live, and bloſſom from the Grave.

LINES,

✝✝✝✝✝✝✝✝✝✝✝✝✝✝✝✝✝✝✝✝✝✝✝✝✝✝✝✝✝✝

L I N E S,

WRITTEN IN THE

POET's CORNER, WESTMINSTER-ABBEY.

———————

WHILE here in labour'd ſtile the marble page

Records each brilliant Genius of the Age,

In awful form the buſt of DRYDEN ſtands,

And, tho' un-epitaph'd, reſpect commands,

A nobler Eulogy his Name conveys,

Than all the Flouriſh, and Lampoon of praiſe,

Our yielding Judgement, like a Magnet, draws,

Adorns the Column, and extorts Applauſe.

Thoſe two plain Words--JOHN DRYDEN--far tranſcend

Whate'er was graven, or whate'er was pen'd.

❖

DESIGN'D

DESIGN'D FOR THE TOMBSTONE

OF A

FRIEND.

LET no rude Hand with impious aim
Deface this monumental Stone.
Wait but awhile, and Time will claim
The Ravage due to him alone.
Then let this small Memorial stand,
Tho' humble, not the less sincere,
Since it was rais'd by Friendship's Hand,
And Pity wash'd it with a Tear.

AN

EPISTLE

TO

Doctor GRAHAM.

ADVER-

ADVERTISEMENT.

TEMPLE *of* HEALTH *and* HYMEN, PALL-MALL.

DR. GRAHAM *desires respectfully to inform the Public, that the New Arrangements and Decorations of this Place being completed, this* ELISIUM *will be open'd this and every Evening next Week ; and that he will have the Honor of delivering from the Celestial Throne, his very celebrated Lecture on Generation—on the Means of exalting, and rendering permanent the temperate and serene Joys of the married State—of preserving youth and personal Beauty and Loveliness—and of prolonging health, full-toned juvenile Virility, and mental Brilliancy, to the longest possible Period of human Existence. The Suite of Apartments in this Elysian Palace—in this magical, enchanting Edifice, far excel, in point of Elegance, Brilliancy, and Magnificence, every Royal Palace in the World ; and to glowing, vivid, and brilliant Imaginations, they will now be found to realize the Celestial, Soul-transporting, and dissolving Descriptions that are given in the Fairy-Tales — in the Tales of the Genii—and in the Arabian Nights Entertainments. In the Course of the Lecture, Dr.* GRAHAM *will un-lock, with Delicacy and Respect, the inmost and sweetest Cabinets of Nature, and he promises, that the Souls of his Auditors, male—mulish, and female, according to their several Capacities and Degrees of Spring, and Sensibility, shall expand, and float, and undulate, through the flowery and airy fields of Elysium, or swim upon ambrosial Oceans of Love and Extasy, to Orbs and Regions of ineffable Bliss.*

EPISTLE

EPISTLE

TO

Doctor GRAHAM.

1.

MAGNIFICENT, and full-toned Sir!
Thou! who haſt made my Pulſe to ſtir
 With more than common Motion,
Beyond what Doctors of the College,
Whoſe Wigs conceal a Fund of Knowledge,
 Can do with Pill, or Potion;

2.

Thou, ſoul-tranſporting Sage! to thee
Quite magic-ſtruck, I bend the Knee,
 Exalt me to thy Band.
There permanent, and fix'd as Fate,
Teach me, like thee, to undulate,
 To float, and to expand.

O

3.

O delicate, respectful King
Of Science! ope my warmest Spring
 Of tickling Sensibility.
Thy firmest Friendship let me prove,
Brilliant—elastic—let me move,
 Transcendent in Agility.

4.

I feel—I feel th' enchanting *Touch*,
A Rapture, that's almost too much,
 For Human Nerves to bear.
Ah! me—I pant—I faint—I die—
But now I glow—burn—vivify—
 And range the Realm of Air.

5.

But quitting your Celestial Bed,
Where Angels have repos'd the Head,
 And your Celestial Throne;
Your Leave I crave with Spirits brisk,
Tho' not electrify'd, to risque
 A Judgément of my own.

Tho'

6.

Tho' Doctors differ in Opinion,
And rule with absolute Dominion,
   In one Point All agree.
Nor from this Practice aught can wean
Their fascinated Minds—I mean—
   The Consultation Fee.

7.

Your System, as it's somewhat New,
Awhile may please the gaping Crew,
   But titillates not all.
Systems of Physic fluctuate,
And, never in one settl'd State,
   Like Stocks, they rise and fall.

8.

When Judgement occupies the Head,
As learned *Radcliffe* well hath said,
   In spite of angry Faction;
True, as the Bias to the Bowl,
Two simple Words include the whole—
   Addition and Sub-traction.

G

The

9.

The plaineſt Things, from Error pure,
Are render'd oftentimes obſcure,
   When Syſtems once begin.
So, Generation turn'd to Science,
To ſet Dame Nature at Defiance,
   Is worth—not worth a Pin.

10.

Without adopting Modes of Art,
When Spirits rage from Part to Part,
   There is a Way to lay 'em.
Thouſands of Mothers have brought forth,
Children of Lovelineſs and Worth,
Who ne'er ſaw *Doctor Graham.*

11.

See the rude Ploughboy, ſtout of Limb,
By Inſtinct guided, not by Whim,
   Or help of any Doctor!
He wants no Spring—no Compaſs He,
To guide his Veſſel through the Sea,
   But is his own Conductor.

12.

Tho' vers'd not in mechanic Pow'rs
He knows, that in her fportive Hours,
    Kind Nature's no Deceiver.
Inform'd by her, he knows his Force,
As a meer Incident of Courfe,
    Depends upon her Lever.

13.

Him nor the Wheel, or Wedge employs,
He longs for more fubftantial Joys,
    All other Joy feems flat.
He leaves the Ballance—Pulley—Screw—
To fuch Philofophers as you,
    And KATTERFELTO's Cat.

14.

Stranger to all the Fairy Tales,
Content with Plains, and Hills, and Dales,
    He needs no fkilful MENTOR.
As Impulfe bids, his Fancy flies,
Like vivid Lightning thro' the Skies,
    Directly to the Centre.

Of

15.

Of fwimming on ambrofial Seas,
Elyfium—floating at one's Eafe,

    What know your Country Loobies!
The Orbs of Blifs to them are *Greek*,
But well they know, whene'er you fpeak,

    Of pretty, pouting Bubbies.

16.

Celeftial Bed—Celeftial Throne,—
And round Virility's full Tone,

    Their Minds in Doubt involve.
But when they meet a willing Maid,
Poor Things! without Defcription's Aid,

    They prefently diffolve.

17.

But canft thou give returning Spunk,
To the dry, wither'd, faplefs Trunk,

    And make old Age to dance,
Or in gay Love's embattl'd Field,
Where Youths of fturdy Prowefs yield,

    Repair his broken Lance?

Thou

18.

Thou canft—elfe wherefore do we fee
Dotards with weak, and trembling Knee,
 Each hobbling to his *Venus!*
Striving full hard to mend their Pace,
And plant a Sort of human Race—
 A *Species* of the GENUS.

19.

For this, thy Praife as long fhall laft,
As youthful Brides, prodigious chafte
 In Thought, in Word and Deed,
Their antique Hufbands Arms forfake,
And to each Ball their Vifits make,
 Or Wat'ring-Place—to breed.

20.

Till Orators of high Renown,
Call'd Statefmen—over-honeft grown,
 Refufe a Place, or Penfion,
Thy Name and Honour fhall remain,
Firm, as the Cloth, that's dyed in Grain,
 And never know Declenfion.

Permit

21.

Permit me now, my Doctor dear!
T' impart a Story to your Ear,
  Not meaning to offend;
Tho' it may damp in some Degree
That artificial Extacy,
  You fain would recommend.

22.

Young HOB, the most athletic Swain,
The archest of the Hob-like Train,
  The Village ever knew,
One Holliday at Country Wake,
His Pastime where he us'd to take,
  Leer'd waggishly at SUE.

23.

SUE was a Lass of brisk Eighteen,
The Lilly and the Rose were seen,
  Twin-Rivals in her Face.
Tho' taught not in the Dancers School,
A natural Ease, uncrampt by Rule,
  Excell'd their stiffen'd Grace.

How

24.

How many Lords, had Lords been there
To view the foft, bewitching Fair,
    And each inviting Dimple,
How many Lords would then have drain'd
Their Privy Purfes to have gain'd
    Admittance to her Temple.

25.

Hob's active Spirits, to and fro',
Like Penny-Poftmen, come and go—
    His ardent Pulfe ran high ;
And, Cæfar-like, he came—he faw—
Determin'd in defpite of Law,
    To conquer, or to die.

26.

Acquaintance made—they danc'd, they fung,
And to each other fondly clung,
    Each was to each a Spur.
Tho' all was Merriment, and Whim,
The clownifh Males all envied him,
    The Females envied her.

Then

27.

Then homeward going, much he prefs'd
Th' alluring Damfel to his Breaft,
 Repeating Kifs on Kifs.
By various Means he ftrove to gain,
By Means I dare not here explain,
 The Region of his Blifs.

28.

Strange Raptures now her Bofom fill,
As thus fhe cry'd—" I'll grant your Will,"
 Hung down her Head, and fmil'd;
" Provided you will give me Leave,
" Your naughty Manhood to bereave,
 " If I fhould prove with Child."

29.

Agreed—fhe clafp'd her ardent Youth,
And, as he vow'd eternal Truth,
 Joy brighten'd ev'ry Feature.
At future Ill fhe was not fhock'd,
But funk compos'd, whilft Hob unlock'd
 The Cabinet of Nature.

The

30.

The Decorations of the Place,
He much admir'd with fimpring Face,
    The New Arrangement—She.
'Twas Blifs ineffable to find
A Swain fo ready to her Mind,
    In Love's extreme Degree.

31.

His *Suaviter in modo*, how
The yielding Fair one might allow,
    I can't prefume to fay.
Of this I'm fure—fhe lik'd full well,
(Th' enfuing Circumftance will tell)
    His *Fortiter in Re.*

32.

At length fhe found her taper Waift,
Like many Belles in high-bred Tafte
    Grow rounder than before.
The blufhing Rofe her Face forfook,
The Lilly the Example took,
    And left her to deplore.
           H.

Enrag'd

33.

Enrag'd a ſharpen'd Knife ſhe drew,
And to the Barn vindictive flew,
  Where Hob diſplay'd his Flail,
" Villain ! you've loaded me with Shame,
" Nor think what Curſes on my Fame
  " You've ventur'd to entail.

34.

" Villain ! for Villain is your Name,
" Prepare yourſelf—I come to claim
  " The Promiſe which you made.
" You've ruin'd me—This Hob well knew—
" And now," ſaid ſhe, " I'll ruin you"—
  And graſp'd the fatal Blade.

35.

Firm as the Giant of the Wood,
Yclep'd an Oak, young Hobby ſtood,
  In Act her Wrath to feel.
His Apparatus when ſhe ſaw,
She felt—a pleaſing Kind of Awe—
  And drop'd the horrid Steel.

36.

" Ah! what fhe cried—what Floods of Blifs
" O'er-whelm my Frame!—A Sight like this,
 " Into a Ferment throws me.
" Tho' its the Spring of all my Woe,
" I cannot meditate a Blow—
 " It looks as if it knows me.

37.

What follow'd, muft not here be faid,
But we'll fuppofe the yielding Maid
 Once more was all content;
For certain 'tis that when fhe came
Forth from the Barn, fhe look'd more tame—
 More pleas'd than when fhe went.

38.

Now DOCTOR! tell, and tell me true,
Speak freely out, as I to you,
 Nor dread the Lafh of Satire;
Can your Celeftial Bed impart
More Joy, or All your Strokes of Art,
 Exceed one Stroke of Nature!

      ODE

ODE to SLEEP.

1.

WRAPT in thy Folds, how sweetly lies
Stout Health, the Son of Exercise,
No hideous dreams his head molest,
But all his Soul's at perfect rest,
Whilst Grandeur with a guilty mind,
In vain would bribe thee to be kind,
And, when his heavy eye-lids close,
Starts up, and trembles at Repose.

2.

O could'st thou in thy leaden Chain
For ever bind each useless Train,
Each sordid avaricious Crew,
What mighty Thanks to thee were due!
For half the World, to whom Distress
In vain applies for kind Redress,
Who live, but for their own dear sake,
Had better be asleep than wake.

PISTUM

PISTUM FARTUM.

(*Anglicé*) A BAK'D PUDDING.

Ode for Music, after the Manner of SWIFT.

RECITATIVO.

PISTUM Fartum well-jumbl'd
By pretty Miſs Rumbold,
Nicely brown'd by that Maiden
Who bakes it, Poll Haydon,

RITORNELLO.

So Haydon and Rumbold
May both be be-jumbl'd,
And Rumbold, and Haydon,
May both be be-laid on.

 Sing Haydon

 Be-laid on,

 And Rumbold

 Be-jumbl'd,

Sing Haydon and Rumbold,
And Rumbold, and Haydon
Be-laid on, be jumbl'd,
Be-jumbl'd, be-laid on.
   DA CAPO.

GOOD

GOOD BREEDING.

A TALE.

READER! if you expect from me,
The trim, the full-dreſt Simile,
Or diction in the pink of Grace,
Burniſh'd with true poetic lace,
Call'd Metaphor, long ſince forſaken,
You'll be moſt woefully miſtaken.

Now 'tis the faſhion for the Muſe,
Inſtead of Proſpects to paint Views,
Calmly ſhe ſits, and will no more
In lofty flights attempt to ſoar;
The roads are made ſo ſmooth and dry,
There's no Neceſſity to fly,
And therefore ſhe has clip'd her wings,
As judging thoſe ſuperfluous things.

'Stead

'Stead of that bold, that wild expreſſion,
Which Fancy keeps in her poſſeſſion,
And all thoſe fine poetic fits,
Which prove the Bard hath loſt his Wits,
Accept a Tale in humble rhime,
We'll play the Bard another time.

GOOD-BREEDING, I had often heard,
Ne'er gave offence in Deed or Word.
A conſtant ſmile ſeren'd her face,
And lent each feature double grace.
The Sweetneſs of her diſpoſition
Could not receive the leaſt Addition.
This Lady then, where-e'er ſhe went,
Diffus'd the Sunſhine of Content.
So ſtudious, and alert to pleaſe,
That all with her were at their eaſe,
To ſpeak in terms more large, and free,
As happy, as they wiſh'd to be.

Tho' nobly born, her noble Birth,
Marr'd not one tittle of her Worth.

That

That Luck, which makes all others vain,
(Proof of some Crack about the Brain,
Which stands in need of so much mending)
Made her more meek, and condescending.
So gentle, and so kind her spirit,
She always took the part of Merit,
Nor e'er would see her once abash'd,
Or as the vulgar call it—dash'd.
For what, as Writers all aver,
Gave others pain, gave more to her,
Keeping this rule before her eye,
Do as you wish to be done by.

With such a frame of Temper blest,
No wonder she was much caress'd.
No wonder I impatient grew,
To have one pleasing Interview,

Oft have I sought this charming Fair,
Now here—in short but ev'ry where,
I've rang'd the Country round and round,
Her Ladyship could not be found.

Oft at Affemblies have I been,
Cockfure, that there fhe might be feen,
But plague on my unlucky Fate!
I always found I came too late.

Oft at an annual Horfe-race Feaft,
I thought to meet this lovely gueft;
But not one gen'rous fon of Adam
Vouchfaf'd to fet a Chair for Madam.
Once in the *Stand*, which Ladies grace,
I caught the Profile of her Face,
Who, e'er I could approach'd her nigher,
Was joftl'd by a Country 'Squire.
Shock'd at the Rudenefs of the Clown,
She took her Coach, and rode to Town.

To London ftrait I bent my way,
Thinking to fpy her at the Play.
I took my ftation in the Boxes,
Where gentle-folks attend by proxies.
A footman, as is oft the cafe,
Supplies the Prefence of his Grace.

I

But

But oh! what interruption here!
What buzzing founds perplex'd the ear!
Believe it truth, nor think it railery,
I wifh'd myfelf in th' Upper Gallery.

I waited next on Man of Quality,
And was receiv'd with much formality.
But by Addrefs I foon was able
To gain Admittance to his Table.
The guefts invited, faving me,
Confifted of no more than three,
A Circumftance, that pleas'd me more,
Than if en-circl'd by a Score.

The firft was call'd a great Phyfician,
The next an able Politician,
The third had gain'd a fund of Knowledge,
By fwallowing Homer at a College,
And never after deign'd to fpeak,
A Sentence, but it clos'd with Greek.

The firft averr'd, as firft in fame,
Sicknefs and Health were not the fame,

And

And clearly prov'd beyond a Doubt,
That enter'd in as *this* went out.
The next harangu'd, and full as **wife**,
On Ways and Means to raife fupplies.
The third pronounc'd his words fo hard,
That J o h n s o n's felf would have been fcar'd.
The Doctor's tedious, technic phrafe,
The Statefman's plans for means and ways,
The humdrum Pedant's ftile **verbofe**,
Rather inclin'd me to a Doze.
In fine—as you may pre-conceive,
I took my Nap, and took my Leave.

To *Rufus* Hall my way I bent,
And to the Courts of Juftice went,
Amus'd myfelf—but why amus'd!
Where **ev'ry** Witnefs was **abus'd**.
Here wrangling Difcord brought forth Crops,
Of Arguments, as thick as Hops,
'Till **each** difputing, knowing Brother
Grew mighty pleafant **on each other.**
Each Term fo apt was, and fo choice,
And utter'd with fo round a Voice,

That

That would have driven to defpair
Buckhorfe, if *Buckhorfe* had been there.
So coarfe each phrafe, I could not ftay,
Nor did I wifh to bring away,
The Epithets of fuch demeanor,
Either the Purport, or the Tenor.

Thought I, the Lady I revere,
And fo much look for, can't be here.
As foon I might expect to fee
A Lawyer's Brief without a fee.
Howe'er I afk'd one precious Limb,
And beg'd to be inform'd by him;
But he refer'd me to *my Lord*,
Who faid fhe was not on Record.

Baulk'd in my Search I mourn'd my hap ill,
And thence repair'd to *Stephen*'s Chapel.
But here Invectives ran fo hot,
That they the Saint had quite forgot.
Let thofe, who think the Tow'r of Babel,
Was nothing more or lefs than Fable,

Come

Come once or twice to thefe Dominions,
They'l change, I warrant, their Opinions.
'Twas vain to look for her I wanted,
Her Intereft was quite fupplanted;
She had feldom paid a Vifit there,
Since ARTHUR ONSLOW left the Chair.
At t'other Houfe I would have knock'd,
But there the Doors were double-lock'd.

'Twas eafy now what courfe to take;
I had but one more pufh to make.
I then determin'd to refort,
As at the firft I ought—to Court.
But how the Devil to get there—
My Coat, as well as Purfe, was bare.
For tho' in profpects from Parnaffus,
No other Country can furpafs us,
And tho' we've good pens, ink, and paper,
Alas! there's not one Woollen-Draper.
Or if there was, there are no Bankers
To give a Draft on for the Spankers.

But to the Purpofe what's all this!
(Excufe this laft Parenthefis)

At

At length I found the Friend I wanted;

I aſk'd a favor—it was granted.

Completely dreſt, away I ventur'd,

And juſt at two th' apartments enter'd.

Perſons beheld I not a few,

Whom long before, and well I knew.

But they had all forgot me quite,

Yet this perhaps might be polite.

With buckram gate, and haughty eye,

Th' embroider'd figures ſtrutted by,

Who not to Company, or reading,

But to their Tailors ow'd their Breeding.

For I remark'd, that who was dreſt

The beſt, was reckon'd bred the beſt.

One Fopling cried—what *Creter's* he!

And look'd directly full at me.

I bluſh'd to find ſuch Treatment here,

And drop'd, unſeen, a ſilent tear.

At length with Joy I ſaw the FAIR.

Whom I had ſearch'd in vain elſewhere,

For ſhe was ſtanding right between

THE KING OF ENGLAND, AND THE QUEEN.

✢ ❀ ✢

THE

THE

COUNTRY GENTLEMAN;

OR,

The CHOICE SPIRITS.

MEN.

FROLIC,
WORTHY,
SWIG, a Landlord.

WOMEN.

ELIZA,
LUCY, her Maid.
Mrs. HARPY.
The CHOICE SPIRITS.

ACT I.

SCENE 1.   A Lodging House.

Enter Landlady, *turning* Eliza, *and her Maid* Lucy *out of door.*

Landlady. GET out of my House—you sha'nt stay another moment.

Eliza. For Heaven's sake—

Lucy. Dear Mrs. Harpy, you surely can't think of turning such a Gentlewoman, as my Lady is, into the Street at this Time of Night.

Landlady. Dont tell me of Gentlewomen and Ladies. I believe you are neither of you better than you should be—'Tis true she paid me very regularly for her Board and Lodging the first three Months; but now here's full five Weeks gone since I saw the Color of her Money.

Eliza. Madam, believe me, I expect Remittances in less than a Week, when you may be assur'd of being satisfied to the utmost Extent of your Wishes.

Landlady. I tell you, I am not to be *flamm'd* in this Manner. Therefore pack off. You'll find some young Spark or other to get you out of this Hobble, I warrant you.

Lucy. This is Language, Madam, my Mistress has never been us'd to.

Landlady. Hold your Tongue, you Baggage! It ill becomes such pert Minxes, as you, to speak to such a *sponsible* House-keeper as I am.

Lucy. Since it comes to that—

Landlady. None of your Sauce, you Trollop! If your Miſtreſs does not bring me *the Cole* To-morrow Morning by Ten o'Clock, I'll break open her Box, and ſell the Contents to the beſt Bidder. So trudge directly.

[*Goes in and flaps the Door to.*

SCENE 2. The *Street.*

Lucy. Trollop indeed!

Eliza. What a Misfortune it is for a Gentlewoman born and bred ſuch, to be in Diſtreſs! It is pitiable even in Gentlemen, but they have many Reſources, which the Delicacy of our Sex will never ſuffer us to ſubmit to.

Lucy. Come, Madam, compoſe yourſelf—I'll never forſake you. 'Tis a fine Moonlight Night, and the Air tolerably warm. As we go, along, we'll conſult on what is proper to be done.

Eliza. Heav'n be my Guard! for, alas! all human Aſſiſtance ſeems to be denied me.

Lucy. Trollop indeed!   [*Exeunt.*

SCENE 3. A *Coffeehouse.*
Enter Frolic *and* Worthy *(meeting.)*

Frolic. Ha—what my old School-fellow, *Freeman.*

Worthy. Worthy, if you pleaſe, *Jack.*

Frolic. What a plague are you aſham'd of your Name!

Worthy. No—but I have chang'd it for a good Eſtate.

Frolic. I give you Joy—Well now, as you are poſſeſs'd of an ample Fortune, I ſuppoſe you intend to take up your Reſidence in Town.

Worthy. Not I indeed—I ſhall ſtill be the ſame, plain, Country Gentleman you ever knew me; and

K   thank

thank Heaven, that I am now enabl'd to do more
Good, than the moderate Income I had before would
possibly allow me.

Frolic. Laughable enough, by all that's waggish.

Worthy. I should think it an ill requital to Provi-
dence, if I suffer'd the Benevolence of my Heart to
be chang'd by any Accession of Fortune.

Frolic. Unfashionable to the last Degree.

Worthy. It may be so—and I am sorry to say that
there are too many Instances in High Life, where
People sprung from the lowest Origin have by some
whimsical Marriages been so elevated with their Suc-
cess, that they have gone pur-blind, and lost their
Memories, the one preventing them from seeing their
old Acquaintance, and the other from knowing their
poor Relations.   It was pleasantly said by a certain
Roman Wag, who on being ask'd his Reason for
wearing a dirty Shirt, replied that his Washerwoman
had lately been made a Countess.

Frolic. Truce with your antiquated Notions—You
had better take a large Mansion at the Court End of
the Town, and keep Half a Dozen Equipages, and
live in a Stile, as a Man of Taste ought to do.

Worthy. Half a Dozen Equipages—What do you
mean?

Frolic. Mean—why I mean as I say—Half a Dozen
Equipages—for ev'ry Tooth-drawer, and Hair-dresser
of Eminence keep one, and surely you would not be so
vulgar as to be on a Level with them.

Worthy. Tooth-drawer, and Hair-dresser of Eminence—I thought the Word Eminence had been con-
fined to some superior Qualities of the Mind.

Frolic. Ha—ha—How little do you know of the
World—Why as the Times go, the Meaning of
Words

Words is totally perverted, and if you take your Opinion from those whom you call the best Authors, and from Dictionaries, you'll find yourself miserably mistaken and meet with nothing, but Laughter and Contempt in and out of ev'ry polite Circle.

Wor. You amaze me.

Frolic. That may be—but it is even so, and you must comply with the Times, or be look'd on as a Creature, an Animal, an insipid Being, that nobody knows, a low Wretch, that never had an Ancestor, one who has——

Worthy. Prithee explain thyself.

Frolic. Don't talk of Explanations—I tell you the Meaning of Words is totally perverted, and few of the Quality ever consult Dictionaries, unless now and then to correct themselves in their Spelling, when they send their Cards of Compliment, or Condolence, tho' that is now render'd useless, as they may be bought of all Sorts and Sizes at so much a Dozen ready engrav'd to their Hands, with only Blanks left to fill up the Names and the Date.

Worthy. This is a Refinement that I was totally unacquainted with.

Frolic. Why I told you before you knew little of the World.

Worthy. By Heav'ns, I would sooner sit down with the meanest Cottager I have than keep such Company.

Frolic. But answer me seriously—Do you really propose spending the Remainder of your Life in the Country?

Worthy. Most seriously, I do.

Frolic. Then I pity you with all my Heart. I would not be confin'd to live there for your whole Estate, where one can have no Company, but a few Upstarts,

who

who knowing nothing, pretend to know every Thing; here and there a Lawyer, who has no more Conscience than an Old Bailey Solicitor, and a lordly Parson, whose Pride fits on the Humility that ought to mark his sacred Character as awkwardly as the Coat of a Giant would on the Shoulders of a Dwarf. There are but two People, whose Friendship I would endeavour to cultivate.

Worthy. Who can they be?

Frolic. The Apothecary and the Barber.

Worthy. Your Reason.

Frolic. The one for fear he should poison me, and the other for fear he should cut my Throat--ha--ha--ha.--

Worthy. You are a strange Fellow.

Frolic. And then you have some over-bearing 'Squires, whose Merit lies in their Purse, who seem to be born for no other Purpose than to kill Game and wear Boots.

Worthy. Not quite so fast--

Frolic. Or else they are eternally ringing Changes, on their Cocks, Horses and Dogs, Dogs, Horses and Cocks, 'till they make one as sick as a Dose of Ipecacuanha.

Worthy. Stop, I beseech you--

Frolic. Or boasting of their Pedigree, tho' they cannot trace it higher than that of one of their Hunters. Strike me comical! if I would not sooner live with a Groupe of Dutch Boors or a Parcel of Hottentots.

Worthy. This is the dark Side of the Picture. I own I have seen the very Reverse of what you have related --'Squires without the least Tincture of Pride, replete with good Humour and Affability, whose Characters would put many a Nobleman to the Blush, Lawyers who are Ornaments to their Profession, and Clergymen

whose

whofe Purity of Manners, and Conduct in Life would have done Honor to the primitive Ages.

Frolic. Come we'll have done with this grave Converfation. It grows late, and I am determin'd to introduce you to a Club of *Choice Spirits* at a Houfe in Holborn.

Worthy. Choice Spirits! who are they?

Frolic. Stars of the firft Twinkle, Sir—Diamonds of the firft Water—Sons of found Senfe and Satisfaction —Brilliants—Jolly Dogs—high mettl'd Fellows, who fain would kick the Globe from underneath their Feet, and tread in Air. Come along with me, for by this Time   [*Sings—to a Tune in the Beggars Opera.*

The Bumpers are charg'd and the Members are met,
The Bottles all rang'd, a Soul-cheering Show,
I'll go in full Glee, and with Rapture forget
In the Landfkip of Mirth the Perfpective of Woe.
Then farewell to Care! to Reflection adieu!
And welcome the Glafs—I'm the better for you.
Whilft the Streamers of Fancy are gayly un-furl'd
O'er the Ocean of Bacchus—A fig for the World.
                                              [*Exeunt.*

SCENE 4.

A Tap-Room in a Public-Houfe. Landlord *in the Bar.*
Enter Frolic *and* Worthy.

Frolic. Well, Dady Swig, how are you?

Swig. Sir, I am proud to fee you.

Frolic. Yes, I knew you was always proud.

Swig. I pray you now—none of your Jokes.

Frolic. Are any of the Company affembl'd?

Swig. Lord, Sir, you are come too foon by an Hour.

Frolic. Since that's the Cafe, what fay you to a Pot of my Landlord's Porter.   *Worthy.*

Worthy. With all my Heart.

Frolic. Is it in good Order, Dady?

Swig. Broight, as a Ruby.

Frolic. And do you hear—let the Pot be clean.

Swig. Shoines like Silver. *Moy Woife* drefs'd her Head by it this Morning inftead of a Looking-Glafs, fhe did. Boy--Boy--make hafte, or I'll warm you.

Frolic. Well Dady, what's your Opinion about Politics? [*Enters Boy with the Porter.*] What *'nifies* any Thing that fuch a poor Ale-houfe Fellow as I *fays,* tho' perhaps I *knows* a Thing or two as well as they who *pretends* to know better—Every one in his Way. You may talk of my Lord this, and my Lord that—'Squire What d'y'call-him, or the Duke of fuch a one—But pepper me like a Welch Rabbit, if I don't heat a Pot of Purl, bake a Toaft, or ftir a Fire with 'em for Five Hundred, and I fay done firft.

Worthy. For Five Hundred—Why then you muft have kept this Houfe many Years to be enabl'd to rifque fo large a Sum.

Swig. Six-and-thirty Years have I liv'd Tenant in this Houfe under——Boy---Boy---fet Candles in the Club-Room---you Dog, you, or I'll warm you. I *thinks I hears* fome of the *Gemmen* coming—But my Bufinefs, Sir, now begins to fall off.

Worthy. How fo?

Swig. All owing to the Removal of the Gallows, Sir, that's all. O that Gallows was always a good Friend to me. The very Sound of it us'd to make my Heart dance for Joy, and now it gives me the Ear-ach.

Worthy. I don't fee how that can affect your Bufinefs.

Swig. Why there it is now—As I faid before, every one in his Way, Sir, every one in his Way. You muft know,

know, that every Collar-day, when the Convicts were carried by my Door, the Houfe was crowded from the Garret to this here Tap-room, and I us'd to take five, fix, and feven Pounds in a Crack. The Froth of the Porter flew about as thick, as Feathers in a Poulterer's Shop. They had better let the Gallows have ftood where it did at the Weft End of the Town.

Frolic. Why fo.

Swig. To put Folks out of Countenance.

Frolic. Why as to that Matter, Dady, I can't fee the Force of your Reafoning, for let it ftand where it will, it is always fure to put the Parties concern'd out of Countenance.

Swig. Befides it fometimes gives one a double Pleafure. I remember when I was a Boy, I went to fee an Execution, and the Place being very much crowded, I gave Two-pence to fit upon the Wall in Hyde Park, and by the greateft good Luck in the World I faw the Men hang'd, and a Soldier fhot at the fame Time. Gemmen—my Service to you—Shall us ha' t'other Pot. I fuppofe you would not like to be *induc'd* to the Club-room before the Prefident takes the Chair.

Frolic. O no—t'other Pot then.

Swig. Boy--Boy--Here fill the Pot, and bring it with a fine, foaming Head.—Well it can't be help'd now, what *'nifies* fretting! [*Boy re-enters*] I hope the next Time the Gallows travels, it will go down to Weftminfter—Set in Cafe it fhould I fhall open a Coffee-houfe, fomewhere near the Hall—You underftand me—where I fhall be glad of your Cuftom.

Frolic. By all Means—but you forgot your Story.

Swig. No Wonder—The Gallows is enough to put ev'ry Thing out of one's Head.

Frolic. You faid you had liv'd fix-and-thirty Years in this Houfe. *Swig.*

Swig. I have fo, as Tenant under his Grace of ——
However I'll name no Names. But he never was the
Man, who ever call'd in for a Pot of Porter in all the
whole Courfe of his *Loife-toime.*

Frolic. Whom do you pay your Rent to ?

Swig. Why to a Man almoft as great as himfelf—to
Mufter Plunder his Steward, and he never comes, but
when he wants Money. He's like the reft of 'em—all
of a Piece, I remember a *Gemman*, who rais'd the
Man, that us'd to fhave him, to the Office of Steward,
and he did fo fhave and trim his Eftate, that at laft the
poor *Gemman*, who was too much of a *Gemman* to look
into his own Affairs, became a Steward to his own Servant. I'll tell you a comical Story, where a *Gemman*
of this Kind had his Eyes open'd at once. Not a
Noculift could have done it better.

Frolic. Do fo--but firft let's pay you, that we may hold
ourfelves in Readinefs for the Company above Stairs.

Swig. Gemmen, I'm *obloig'd* to you. There was a
Quaker, who had a fnug Eftate, and all he wanted, was
to buy a little Clofe, that ftood in the Middle of it be-
longing to *'Squire Wealthy.* He was willing to give the
full Worth of it, or more, but had heard that *Mufter
Pillage*, (firft Coufin to *Mufter Plunder* who I told you
of before) wanted it for another Perfon, tho' in fact it
was for himfelf. Inftead therefore of going to *Mufter
Pillage*, he goes in his Abfence to the 'Squire himfelf,
and offer'd him the full Value of it, and he *deferr'd*
him to *Pillage.* On which the Quaker ftared him full
in the Face, Sir, as I do you, and faid " I beg thee
Pardon, Friend, I thought the Clofe had been thine
own." This fo ftagger'd the 'Squire, that he began
to doubt whether it was or not. At laft recollecting
that it was, he bargain'd with the Quaker, and fo the
Steward was left in the Lurch. *Frolic.*

Frolic. Well, but, Dady, it is almoft Time to go up Stairs. What Fun is going forward to Night? Is there to be any good Singing.

Swig. That's juft as it happens---But you fhould have been here the other Night Sir. There fat a Fellow in that Box, who fung the *hoigheft*, the *broighteft*--- You may talk of your Playhoufe *Quivering*, or your *Opera* hard Names, but they are no more to be compar'd to him than a Whiftle-pipe to a Trumpet---Six Foot *hoigh*,---ftrait as a Dart---You might heard him up to the Top of *Snow-Hill*.

Worthy. Well but, Landlord, I hope you don't intend to go into the Club-room with your Nightcap on.

Swig. Indeed but I *does*, and why not.

Worthy. I fhould imagine the Company would think you was going to Bed.

Swig. Lord help you, Sir, I fee you are but a Greenhorn: I knows my Men, and they *knows parfitly* well, that *Swig* will have his Way. No, Sir, when I *wears* a Wig, I *wears* a Wig, I *does*---none of your Guinea or Five-and-twenty Shilling Touches---Five Guineas Sir---nothing under---Curls, Tier above Tier---fomething--a--a--a--a--a--fomething Churchwardenical.

Frolic and *Worthy.* Ha--ha--ha--

Frolic. Why really you have a good inventive Faculty.

Swig. I never *troubles* my Head about the Faculty, not I. No Sir; here's my Noftrum, *(grafping the Pot.)* Here's my Julep---beats all the Drops and *Neffences* of the Shops—I have as good a Conftitution now as I had 40 Years ago, and Lungs like a Game-Cock —Ton ta--Ton ta--Ton ta--Ton ti--Ton-tonti---Ton ---Ton tonti--Ton ta---In hoics---In hoics--Hoo--in-- in--in--in--in--

L

Worthy.

Worthy. Upon my Word, you would make a good Huntſman.

Swig. Hunting---No Man upon the Face of the whole total *varſal Yearth* loves the Sport, better than I *does*; and if it was not *Noight*, I would bring my Hunter into the Room to ſhew you. I *rides* five-and-twenty *Moile* to throw off, and before I *mounts* him, the poor dumb Thing is ſo proud to ſee me, that he turns round, and ſniggers in my Face; and when I am firmly ſeated, he turns round, and ſniggers at me again, he *does*, as much as to ſay *Muſter Swig*, I am pleas'd with my lovely Burden.

Frolic and *Worthy.* Ha--ha--ha.

Enter Boy.

Boy. Sir, The Chairman's come, and deſires you will ſend up two Bowls of Punch, directly.

Swig. Then, Gemmen, you'll excuſe me—Follow me—I'll *induce* you—I'll *induce* you.

[*Exeunt.*

End of Act I.

ACT II.

SCENE 1. *A Club-Room with* 20 *or* 30 *ſitting at a long Table, with Pipes and Tobacco, &c.*

Enter Swig, Frolic, *and* Worthy.

Swig. Mr. Chairman—Two freſh Members.

Chairman. Ah, Dady! I ſee you are a Wag—What I ſuppoſe you thought the Houſe wanted freſh Members—a certain Proof that you was tir'd of the old ones——(A general Laugh.)

Swig. Old or new, it's all the ſame Thing to me, if I can but gain my Point, and make up a Reckoning—(Another Laugh.)

Chair.

Chairman. Come bring the Punch, that we may begin upon Bufinefs.

Swig. Bring directly.—Boy--Boy.

[*Swig goes out, and re-enters with two Bowls.*

Chairman. Gentlemen, are you all charg'd.

Many fpeaking at once. All charg'd, moft noble!

Chairman. Then I'll give you a Sentiment---Here's the two Impoffibilities.

(All drink.)

A Member at the **lower** *End of the Table half intoxicated before he came in.* Ex---explain.

Chairman. **Love** without Fear, and Life without **Pain.**

The laft Member. Love without Life, and Fear without Pain. (Hiccups.) Aye, that's about equal to one of my worft---(hiccups.)

Chairman. Come, Gentlemen, a Bumper---Give me a Toaft. [*fpeaking to his Right-hand Man.*

Right-hand Man. The two Strangers at Court.

Chairman. The two Strangers at Court.

A Member. Who can **they** be? Two foreign Ambaffadors, I fuppofe.

Another. No, you Block-head---Honor and Honefty.

Another, Aye---then I am fure, they can have no Bufinefs there, for who, do you think would introduce two fuch poor Devils?

Chairman. Is the Toaft gone round.

One and all. It is, moft noble.

Chairman. Then Silence, Gentlemen, for a Song from Mr. *Jenkins.*

Song,

Song, *by Mr. Jenkins.*

ABOUT Coalition let's wrangle no more,
Since it brings us a durable Pleasure in Store,
Let the Lords and the Commons against me unite,
What they fancy is wrong, I will prove to be right.
Derry-down.

Without Coalition would Fancy decay,
Nor Females their Charms to Advantage display.
The Blending of Tints adds a Sweet to the Sweet,
And the Light & the Shade make the Picture complete.
Derry-down.

Without Coalition what Music would please!
All flat, or all sharp, to enrapture would cease.
The Sameness of Tone we all treat with Neglect;
'Tis the Union of Parts, that produces Effect.
Derry-down.

The Spring, Summer, Autumn, and Winter severe,
In Harmony's Dance join to perfect the Year.
Take one from the four, only one from the Train,
The Link, when once broken, would sever the Chain.
Derry-down.

Should this Definition appear to be tame,
Too trifling to praise, or too worthless to blame,
I'll give you one more, which you all must approve,
And that's—the well-form'd Coalition of Love.
Derry-down.

May there be all happy—Come, brimmer the Glass,
And let the gay Toast in full Merriment pass.
To please, and be pleas'd, let us do what we can,
And Marriage accomplish, what Courtship began.
Derry-down.

Bravo—

Bravo—Bravo—Bravo—[*from one End of the Table.*

Tippy toppy, tippy toppy, tippy toppy,—[*from the other End.*

Chairman. Charge---Here's the *Coalition* of Love, and then drink *ad libitum* as the *Muficianers* fay, and let us kill Time as faft as we can.

A Member. That's right, my Boy, for we know Time will kill us, if we don't kill him.

Another. That's a good one---let you alone for a Piece of Wit.

Worthy. Frolic! What are you whifpering to your next Neighbour about?

Frolic. I was only afking about *Jack Rattle*---a fine, pimple-nofed Spirit, who us'd to be the Fiddle of the Company, and would touch up an extempore Song, while you could fay *Jack Robinfon*---A Member of moft of the Societies in London, and keeps the beft Company.

Worthy. O ho! I now begin to perceive the Truth of what you afferted to me Half an Hour ago---That the Meaning of Words is totally perverted---for if I may judge, from what I fee, the beft Company is the worft.

Frolic. He was the Crack of the Town, and Treafurer of a famous Charitable Club, but unfortunately the other Night he ran away with the Box that held the Money, and is now in Tothill-fields Bridewell to be carried before the Juftices To-morrow, but he is a very honeft Fellow at Bottom. Great Men are fubject to Misfortunes, as well as little ones.

Worthy. You have a fine Way of reafoning, and of reconciling Matters.

Frolic. Stop---there's a Gentleman going to fpout a fublime Soliloquy out of a Tragedy, which he has

lately

lately written himfelf, and which the Managers have rejected, not from its Want of Merit I affure you (for I wrote Half a Scene in it myfelf) but meerly, becaufe the Houfe was over-ftock'd——

Worthy. With Senfe, do you mean?

Frolic. No--No--With Plays; that is--with tragical Comedies, and comical Tragedies.

> (*A Member gets up to fpeak—A general Hubbub, with a Cry of Waiter--Waiter--More Punch. A frefh Paper of Tobacco. Tinkle the Jingler.---Then Silence, Silence. Order--Order--Hear him--hear him——*)

Member fpeaks.

O that my Lungs could bleat, like butter'd Peas,
And eke in bleating catch the venom'd Itch,
Or grow as mangey as the Irifh Seas,
To engender Whirlwinds on a Lapland Witch!
Not that a hard-roed Herring dare prefume,
To fwing a Tithe-pig in a Cat-fkin Purfe;
Becaufe that the late Hailftones which fell at Rome
By leffening their Fall would make it worfe.
I grant that drunken Rainbows lull'd to fleep
Snort, like Welch Hooks, in a fair Lady's Eyes,
Which made him laugh to fee a Pudding creep,
For creeping Puddings always pleafe the wife.
The Reafon's plain, for Charon's Weftern Barge,
Running full Tilt 'gainft the fubjunctive Mood,
Beckon'd to Bagley-Park, and gave a Charge,
To fatten Padlocks with Antartic Food.

> (*All clap, and cry bravo.*)

Frolic to Worthy. Well my Friend, what fay you to this Specimen! Do you think any modern Author befides him can write fo?

Worthy. Not, 'till he has been confin'd at leaft fix Months in Bedlam.

The

The Speaker. Ha---what's that the Gentleman fays?

Frolic. He highly approves of the Paffage, and fays he is well acquainted with one of the Managers, and will ufe his Intereft in your Behalf.

The Speaker. (*Starting up in a Rapture, and advances to Worthy.*) Sir, I am your moft obedient humble Servant.---I fee, Sir, you are a Man of Tafte, and if you will do me the Honor of calling on me at my Lodgings To-morrow Morning—Here, Sir, is my Addrefs (*giving a Card*) I will read the whole Tragedy to you.— Perhaps, Sir, you little think to what I am indebted for the Loftinefs of the Speech you have juft heard me repeat.

Worthy. Why, really Sir, I can afcribe it to nothing elfe than a copious Libation of Burgundy.—I own it was a happy flight.

Speaker. Happy flight---Egad you have hit it.---It was a happy flight; for you muft know I wrote it in an Air Balloon.

Worthy. Indeed!

Speaker. Upon my Honor. You cannot conceive the Difference between writing in the Air, where one is plac'd fo much above the World, and fcribling upon this grov'ling Element the Earth—Here the Ideas are ob-nubilated—abfolutely bound up in total Condenfation, like fo many Cakes of Ice.---But there they fparkle, vivify, and expand, rarify with Celerity, melt into Liquidity, and float with Hilarity.—But we'll not interrupt the Bufinefs of the Night.—To-morrow I expect you.--Sir your moft obedient humble Servant-- (*whifpering*)---Not a Word of the Balloon.

Worthy. O no.

Speaker. Becaufe if my Brother Authors fhould get hold of the Idea, they will improve upon the Princi-

ple,

ple, and outfail me---perhaps take a Trip to the Moon, and rake out fome of the Combuftibles from the Burning Mountain, hurl 'em at my Head, and make my Story in fome Meafure a Counterpart to the Fall of *Phaeton.*

Chairman. Silence, Gentlemen, for a *Duette* between Mr. *Hooknofe* and *Tom Warble.*

Frolic. Now, you fhall hear fomething capital---fine Voices---only they are apt to knock the King's Englifh about.

Worthy. Knock the King's Englifh about---I don't underftand you.

Frolic. It's a particular Phrafe, and means an Inaccuracy of Expreffion, or in other Words they don't mind facrificing Senfe to Sound. I fancy they borrow'd it from the Italian School.

Chairman. Silence Gentlemen, or I fhall call for a Tumbler of Salt and Water.

Duette between Mr. Hooknofe and Tom Warble.

WHEN Phœbe the Tops of the Hills do adorn,
How fweet is the Sound of the ecchoing Morn!
When the mantling Stag is arouz'd by the Sound,
Neglecting his Ears, nimbly creeps o'er the Ground,
And thinks he has left us behind on the Plain,
But ftill we purfue, now and then come in View
Of the glorious Game.
Oh! fee how again, how his Ears and his Head,
And winged for fear, he is troubl'd with Speed;
But ah! 'tis in vain, 'tis in vain that he tries,
That his Legs lofe the Huntfman, his Ears lofe their Eyes,
For now his Strength fails him, he heavily flies,
    And he pants,
Till with well-centre Hounds all confounded he dies.
          [*Here a Roar of Applaufe.*]
                              Hooknofe.

Hooknose. I call for a Song from the Chair.

Warble. No---No,---let him give us the Puppet-
fhow.

All. **Aye,** aye, the Puppet-fhow, the Puppet-fhow.

A Member. All you who are of Opinion that he ought
to give us the Puppet-fhow, fay Aye.

All. **Aye---aye.**

Member. All you who are of a contrary Opinion,
fay No. The Ayes have it.

Chairman begins. The firft Figure, Gentlemen and
Ladies, that I fhall fhew you is **Punch** and his Merry
Family. Why don't you bring 'em out there : *(Afide
and changing his Voice, as if anfwer'd by a Companion.)*
They are gone into the Country to canvafs for a vacant
Borough. Why then fend in the Bench of Juftices,
with the Chairman at their Head.---It's all the fame.
---The Gentlemen will excufe it. Tol lol lol lol.---
*(To any Tune that occurs, playing on two Pipes by way of
Fiddle.)*

The next Thing that I fhall fhew you is, **The Mayor**
and Court of Aldermen.---Send 'em there *(changing
his Voice as before.)* They are juft fet down to Sup-
per, and you may as well attempt to remove the Mo-
nument.---Why then fend in the fatted Calves, and
the thick-headed Drover from Effex.---It will do---the
Gentlemen will excufe it. Tol lol lol---

Now, Gentlemen, I fhall fhew you two monftrous
fine Figures indeed---St. George and the Dragon.---
Obferve and take Notice of the Figure of St. George,
the Richnefs of his **Drefs,** the fharp-pointed Lance in
his Hand---the Glare of the Dragon's Eye-balls---the
Latitude of his Mouth, and the Longitude of his
Tail---There's a Tail, if you talk of a Tail---Send in

St. George and the Dragon. *(Changing his Voice.)---*
What fignifies expofing yourfelf—You know you never
had half Money enough either to buy one or the other.
—Why then fend in the Sandman and his Jackafs---It
will do. Tol lol lol, &c.

A drunken Member. This is fuch d--a--a--m'd Stuff,
there's no bear--(hiccups) bearing it. Come---I--I--I'l
give you a Song of my own ma--making, (hiccups.)

Chairman. You Rafcal ! what do you mean by inter-
rupting me.—There take that, *(flinging a Pipe at his
Head.)*

[*A general Uproar, and feveral ftrip to fight.*

Enter two Bailiffs and arreft the Chairman.

Bailiff. So I have nabb'd you at laft, Mr. Merry-
man.—Come you fhall go along with us—You fhall
have your Belly-full of Punch at my Houfe—that is
if you have Money to pay for it, (afide.)

[*During this Confufion,* Frolic *and* Worthy *walk
off, and the Scene changes to an adjacent Street.*]

Frolic. This laft Scene was rather difagreeable, but
I'll make **you** ample Amends, if you will go with me
to the *Devil.*

Worthy. Not a Step farther—I keep much better
Company at the *Angel.* I have had enough of Fun,
as you call it ; and am forry to fee a Man of your
Education proftitute his Time and Talents in fo con-
temptible a Manner.

Frolic. Pfhaw—you have no Life in you—no Spunk.
You are as dull as a Weeping-Willow.—Balloon me,
if you are not grown an arrant Humdrum, and move

in

in as narrow a Compaſs as a Bee in a Jug.—And ſo
good Night to you, for if I ſtay longer I ſhall catch
the Infection, which I would not do for all the dirty
Acres you are poſſeſs'd of—Ha--ha--ha.--

Enter Eliza *and* Lucy.

Worthy. Ha—what do I ſee here.—This Lady by
her Form and Air muſt be a Perſon of Conſequence.
Un-hackney'd as I am in the Ways of Women, I'll
venture to ſpeak to her. Madam——

Eliza. Pray, Sir, forbear, and leave me to my Reflections.

Worthy. Madam, I am ſorry to ſee you ſo dejected,
and if you will do me the Favor to communicate your
Diſtreſſes, you ſhall find me your Friend. For I think
there is no Pleaſure on this Side the Grave, equal to
that of having the Will and the Power of doing good.
There is ſomewhat in your Deportment Madam, that
highly intereſts me in your Behalf, and if I am not
impertinent, pray oblige me with your Story, and you
ſhall find me a Man of Honor.

Eliza. Since you are ſo very frank, Sir, I will tell
you in a few Words.——Know then, Sir, I was born
and bred a Gentlewoman. My Father is Sir *Thomas
Acreman,* in the Weſt of England, and becauſe I will
not conſent to marry a rich Acquaintance of his, old
enough to be my Grandfather, he has totally diſcarded
me. He knows at the ſame Time that my Heart is
previouſly engag'd to a young Clergyman of the Name
of *Heartwell,* who poſſeſſes but a ſmall Benefice, and
on Account of my Attachment to him my Father re-
fuſes to give me a Shilling. Not knowing what to do,

I

I fled to London, thinking to find Refuge with a Lady of my Acquaintance, but unfortunately she had set off for France two Days before my Arrival. I have waited for her Return 'till my little Finances are quite exhausted; and the Woman of the House, where I lodge, has turn'd me out of Doors, and if I do not pay her by To-morrow Morning, says she will break open my Box, and sell the Contents to the Best Bidder.

Worthy. Be comforted Madam. Heav'n in the End is sure to reward Virtue in Distress. This is a fortunate Circumstance, I too, Madam, live in the West of England, about 40 Miles distant from your Father, to whose Name I am not a Stranger. The Mr. *Heartwell* you speak of was my Fellow-Collegian. I am glad I have found him out, and will assist you both in your intended Union. I am intimately acquainted with an opulent Gentleman who has great Influence over your Father, and I make no doubt of the Conclusion of an Event, that will make you, and my Friend *Heartwell* happy. In the mean Time, Madam, do me the Honor of accepting this, *(giving a Bank Note,)* to discharge the Demand on you. Take a Hackney-Coach To-morrow Morning, and drive to my Lodgings, which you will find in this Address *(giving a Card)* and I will take you down to my Seat, and place you under the Care of my Sister, till Matters are adjusted to your Satisfaction.

Eliza. Your Goodness, Sir, quite over-whelms me. My Heart is too full for Utterance.

Worthy. Dry up your Tears Madam, and I will attend you safe to your Door, and protect you by the Way from any rude Assault.——And now, as I have
begun

begun my Career well, I am determined to finiſh it in the ſame Manner. I care not for the Remarks of the diſſipated, or the frivolous Part of Mankind.— Whilſt I have the Satisfaction of my own Breaſt, I am indifferent to Cenſure. And the ſenſible elegant POPE, as he has been judiciouſly ſo call'd, was never more right in his Life, than when he aſſerted

" One ſelf-approving Hour whole Years out-weighs

" Of ſtupid Starers, and of loud Huzzas."

E N D.